Eye on Invention

Written by Lynette Evans

U.S.A.

My name is Peter. I live in the United States. Some important things, such as electric light and voice recording, were invented in my country. Can you think of any other inventions that have improved life around the world?

Contents

A World of Inventions	4
Bright Sparks	6
A Wizard at Work	8
In the Workplace	10
Around the Home	12
On the Move	14
Keeping in Touch	16
Showtime!	18
Simple Successes	20
For the Record	22
Find Out More!	24
Index	24

Look for the Activity Zone!
When you see this picture, you will find an activity to try.

A World of Inventions

Take a look at all the things around you that have been made by people. Many of them are products or devices that smart-thinking people have dreamed up to make life easier, safer, faster, or more enjoyable.

Inventions happen when people try to solve a problem in a new way. To come up with an idea, inventors combine creative thinking with the basic rules, or principles, of science. Every invention brings new knowledge to the world.

device a small machine used for a particular purpose

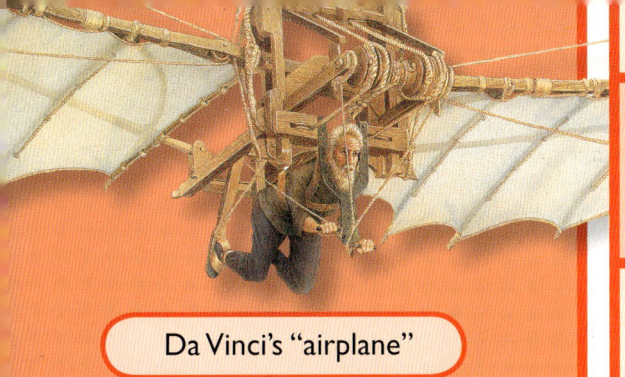

Da Vinci's "airplane"

Leonardo da Vinci was a great inventor who lived in the 1400s. He had ideas for machines that we have only had the technology to build in modern times.

technology scientific knowledge in areas such as engineering

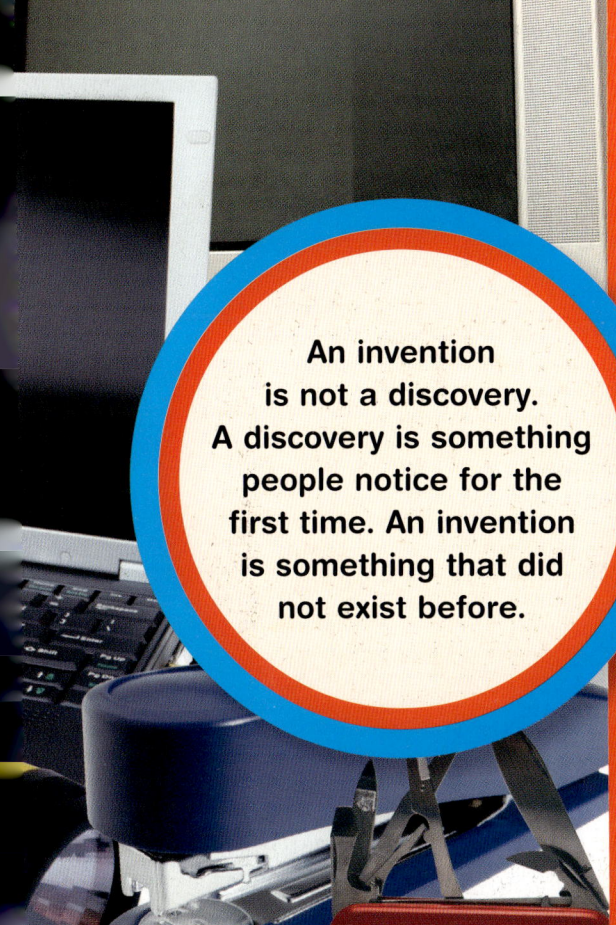

An invention is not a discovery. A discovery is something people notice for the first time. An invention is something that did not exist before.

Activity Zone!

Think of an invention that would make your life easier or more fun.

1. Draw your invention or build a model. What materials will you need?

2. Make up a name for your invention.

3. Design a poster advertising your invention.

What existing technologies did you use for your new idea?

Bright Sparks

Inventions have changed the way people around the world work, play, move about, and communicate. Inventions have come from all times in history and from all parts of the world. During the 1800s in America, however, it seemed that inventions were happening in almost every backyard, basement, and workshop across the land. This time is known as the "great age of American invention." From it arose life-changing inventions such as the electric light bulb, the telephone, and the airplane.

communicate   to exchange information

Scientist and Inventor

Ralph Waldo Emerson was a famous American writer. In 1870, he wrote that "invention breeds invention." What do you think he meant?

Benjamin Franklin (1706–1790) is honored today as one of America's founding fathers and most widely successful citizens. His many interests included science and invention. He always wanted to understand how things worked. This led him to invent all sorts of things, such as the lightning rod. He attached a metal rod to the top of a building. Instead of hitting the building, lightning hit the rod and was drawn down a wire into the earth, protecting the building.

In 1752, Benjamin Franklin showed that lightning is an electric current. He tied a metal key to a kite and flew it during a storm. Lightning hit the kite, and sparks flew off the key. He probably did not hold the string, however, as this would have given him a deadly electric shock.

A Wizard at Work

The American scientist Thomas Alva Edison patented more than a thousand inventions. He set up an invention factory in New Jersey, where he became known as "the Wizard of Menlo Park."

One of Edison's main goals was to figure out a practical way of using electricity to produce light. In 1879, after 9,000 experiments, Edison invented the electric light bulb. In 1882, he opened a power station in New York, and before long similar power stations were supplying electricity across America.

Later in life, Edison was honored for his inventions. However, when light bulbs first lit up the streets, farmers worried that the light would keep their cows awake at night!

patent to acquire the official right to be the only person allowed to make and sell an invention

Power to the People

"Genius is one percent inspiration and 99 percent perspiration."
—Thomas Edison

Electricity has to be sent from the power station where it is made to the homes and businesses where it is used.

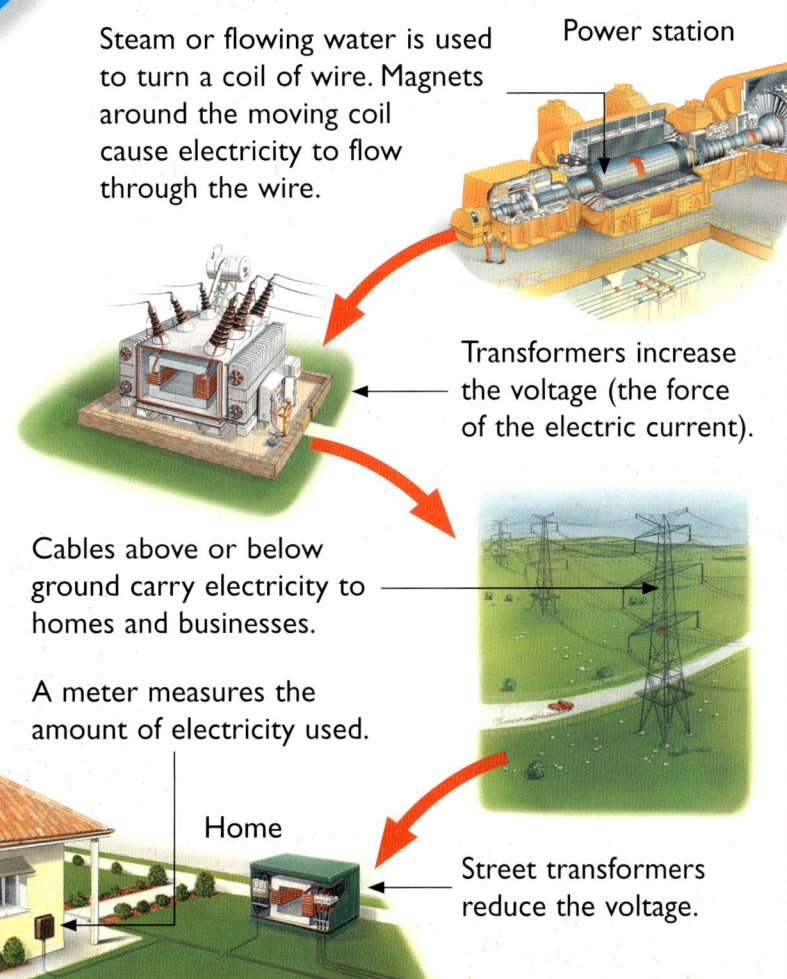

Steam or flowing water is used to turn a coil of wire. Magnets around the moving coil cause electricity to flow through the wire.

Power station

Transformers increase the voltage (the force of the electric current).

Cables above or below ground carry electricity to homes and businesses.

A meter measures the amount of electricity used.

Home

Street transformers reduce the voltage.

Some light bulbs contain a thin, coiled wire, called a *filament*, which heats up and glows when an electric current flows through it.

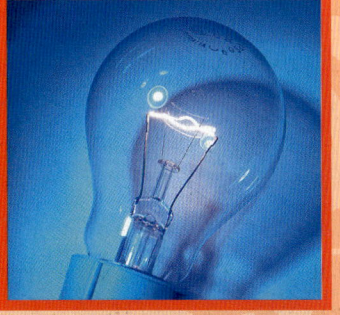

In the Workplace

Wherever people work—in offices, factories, and farms—inventions now make their jobs faster and easier than in the past. Some inventions are machines or other useful objects, and some are processes, or new ways of doing things.

During the 1800s, farmers were the largest group of workers in America. George Washington Carver, an African-American scientist and inventor, revolutionized farming in the southern states when he showed that poor soil could be made productive again by planting a crop of peanuts.

Carver spent much of his time teaching African-American students about science and invention.

revolutionize   to make a great change to something

Faster and Cheaper

> The typewriter was invented in the 1860s. It had a huge impact on office workers. What invention has replaced it today?

In 1798, an American inventor named Eli Whitney developed the process of mass production used in factories to this day. American car manufacturer Henry Ford later invented a moving assembly-line system using conveyor belts to bring parts to the workers. These inventions allowed people to produce large quantities of goods in less time.

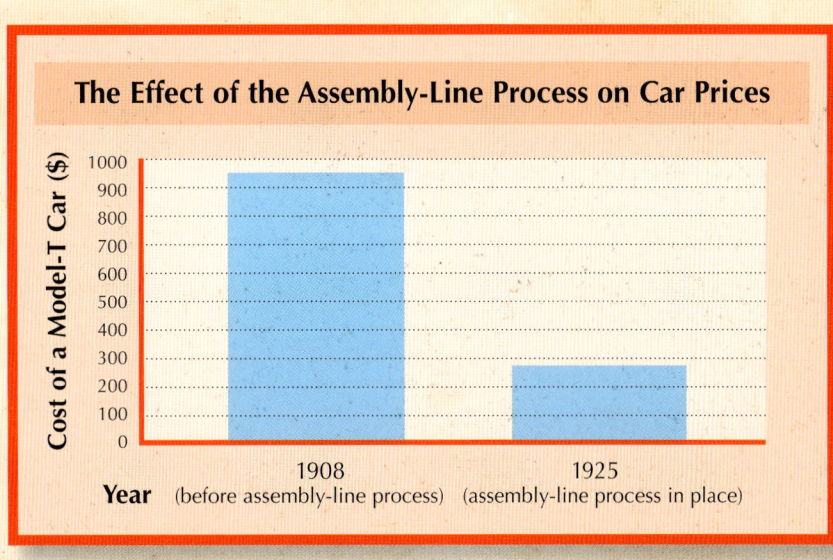

The Effect of the Assembly-Line Process on Car Prices

mass production   when many items of the same kind are made all at once

Around the Home

Most of the labor-saving inventions used in the home are electric machines. These inventions have taken the effort out of many household chores.

Before the electric washing machine was invented, doing the laundry took all day—and that did not include the ironing! Before the vacuum cleaner came along, it took many hours of hard work to beat the dust out of carpets. Today, machines such as dishwashers and refrigerators make our lives easier and give us more time to do other things.

Early electric washing machines were seen as great labor-saving devices. However, clothes still had to be threaded through a dangerous wringer to remove the water.

How Things Work

A vacuum cleaner works in a way similar to a straw. When you drink through a straw, you suck out the air, and this draws up the liquid. A vacuum cleaner creates a powerful flow of air that sucks up dust through a hose and traps it inside the machine.

A microwave oven cooks food very quickly. It uses powerful energy waves that penetrate food to heat it from the inside and the outside at the same time.

penetrate   to go into something

Before electric refrigerators, people had to shop for fresh food most days.

In 1846, Elias Howe invented the world's first sewing machine. It made this age-old task far easier.

13

On the Move

It is hard to imagine life without trains, cars, and airplanes. However, many everyday methods of transportation were invented only in the last few centuries. The first steam-powered boat traveled up the Hudson River from New York City in 1807. Soon, huge steamships were crossing the oceans. Over the years, the bicycle, the train, and later the automobile enabled people to travel faster and farther across land. In 1903, the Wright brothers from Ohio invented the airplane, and the age of flight began.

transportation a means of moving people or things to another place

How Planes Fly

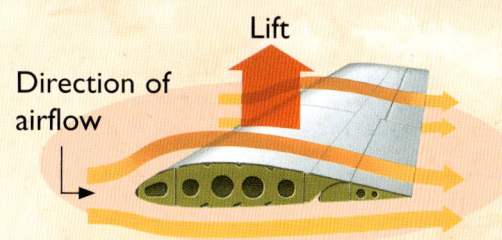

The study of how air flows around objects is called *aerodynamics*. Air does not flow easily around wide, sharp-edged shapes, but it does flow easily around slim, smoothly curved shapes. Many of today's streamlined trains, airplanes, and cars are designed using aerodynamics.

streamlined something with a sleek, smooth shape that air flows over easily

The wings on an airplane are a special shape called an *airfoil*. Air passing over the curved top of the wing travels faster than air traveling under its flatter base. The slower air underneath puts more pressure on the wing than the faster air, and this pressure pushes the wing upward.

Birds' wings are also airfoil shaped.

Blow fast air over the top of a strip of paper. The paper will lift just like an airplane wing.

The Changing Bicycle

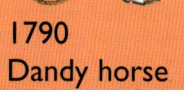 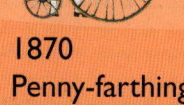  

1790 Dandy horse   1870 Penny-farthing   1879 Safety bike   1980s Aerodynamic bike

Keeping in Touch

At an invention fair in 1876, a man named Alexander Graham Bell showed a new device that enabled voice messages to be transmitted along a wire almost instantly. Bell's "speaking telegraph," or telephone, was an immediate success. Later, other inventors, such as Thomas Edison, improved the telephone, making it easier to use.

Today, computers connect people to a worldwide web of information. Words, sounds, and images are sent to homes and businesses around the world within seconds.

transmit to send something from one place to another

The personal computer (PC) was developed in the U.S. in 1975. However, few families owned computers until the 1990s.

In a telephone earpiece, an electric signal goes into a loudspeaker. The loudspeaker changes the signal into vibrations that sound just like the speaker's voice.

In the mouthpiece, the vibrations caused by a person's voice are used to create an electric signal, which travels down the wire.

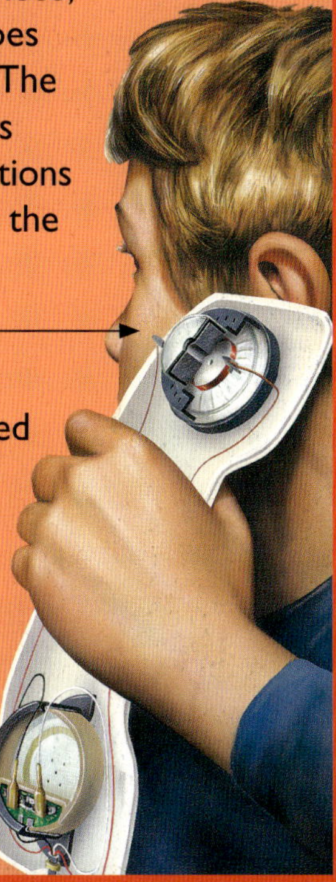

Telegraph Messages

American Samuel Morse was the first to invent a practical way of sending a message along a wire. In 1844, he used a magnet to alter the flow of electricity in a wire and create a beep at the other end. Patterns of long and short beeps were used to spell words.

Morse Code

A •−	B −•••	C −•−•	D −••
E •	F ••−•	G −−•	H ••••
I ••	J •−−−	K −•−	L •−••
M −−	N −•	O −−−	P •−−•
Q −−•−	R •−•	S •••	T −
U ••−	V •••−	W •−−	X −••−
Y −•−−	Z −−••		

Decode this message to see why Morse code was so important.

•−− •− − −•−• ••••   −−− ••− −

•••• −−− •−• ••• •   − •••• •• • ••−•

−−− −•   •−− •− −−•−

17

Showtime!

The telephone was an invention that put individuals in touch with one another. Then, when radio shows and movies came on the scene during the 1920s, huge numbers of people were able to share in the same events and enjoy common experiences. Radio waves beamed news, information, and entertainment into homes. In America, especially, the movies captured the imagination of millions, and theaters opened across the nation.

The first movies had no sound. Instead, music was played to create atmosphere.

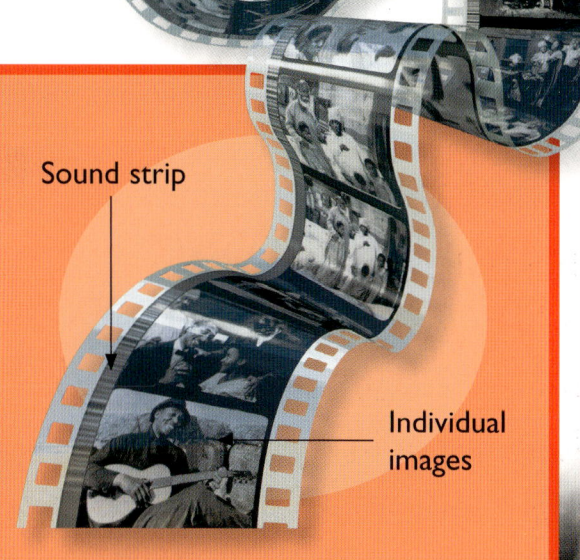

Sound strip

Individual images

Film is made up of many photographs taken one after another. When viewed very quickly, they appear to show one moving image.

A sound strip runs alongside the film. This ensures that the words match people's mouth movements.

A Trick of Technology

Television programs are transmitted by underground cables or radio waves. Cables carry electrical signals. Radio waves are picked up by an antenna and changed into electrical signals. The television then changes the signals into pictures and sound. It produces three beams of electric particles, called *electrons*, that light up different parts of the screen.

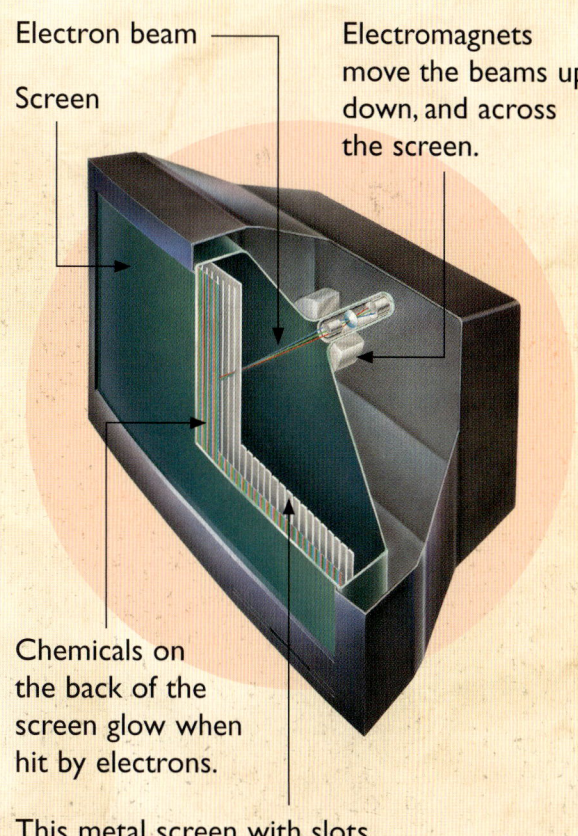

Electron beam

Screen

Electromagnets move the beams up, down, and across the screen.

Chemicals on the back of the screen glow when hit by electrons.

This metal screen with slots ensures the electron beam hits the right part of the screen.

Simple Successes

Not all inventions are big, earthshaking events. Many of the most successful and useful inventions are simple items that have made people's lives easier or more comfortable. We use zippers, toothbrushes, sunglasses, self-stick notes, umbrellas, and other inventions every day. Many simple inventions have remained unchanged over the years. Others are innovations, inventions that use new materials and technologies to improve an existing idea. The electric toothbrush is an innovation.

In 1886, New Yorkers invented a new word. It came about when Frenchman Monsieur Gaget started selling tourists tiny models of the Statue of Liberty. People called these models "gadgets." Today, the word is used to describe any simple, yet clever, device.

All inventions need a name. The umbrella is an age-old invention. It was first used as a sunshade in ancient China. The name comes from a Latin word that means "little shadow."

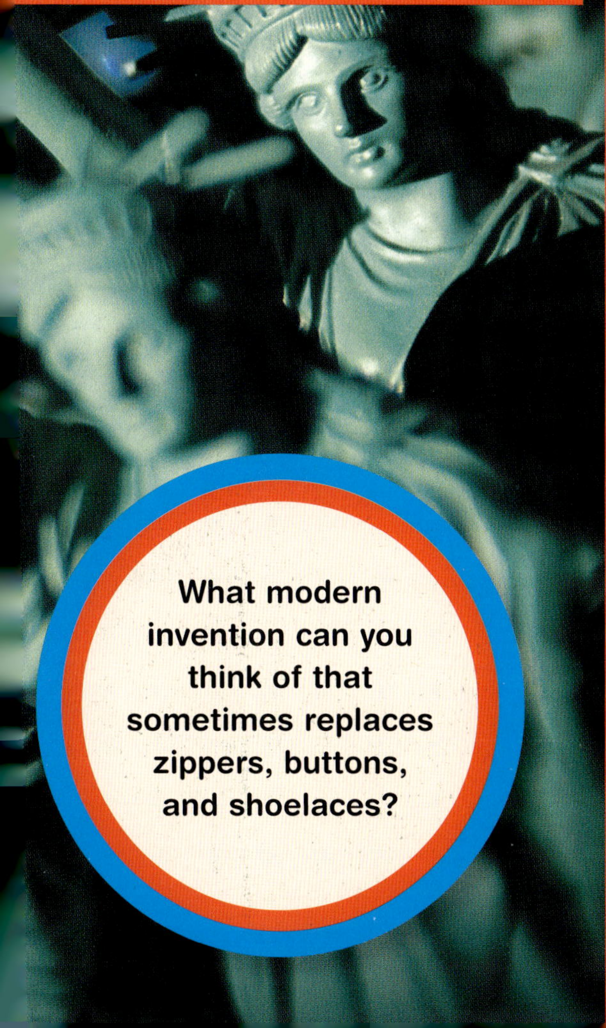

A Young Inventor

Kids have some of the most inventive minds on the planet! When Rachel Kaminsky from Ardsley, New York, was eight years old, she invented the Dry Eyes Onion Slicer (above) and won the regional first prize in the Young Inventors Awards Program. The next year, she was one of ten national finalists in the same awards program when she invented The Shoe Lace Helper, a device that helps children learn to tie their shoelaces.

What modern invention can you think of that sometimes replaces zippers, buttons, and shoelaces?

For the Record

If an inventor patents a new idea, he or she can earn money from people who use the invention. Inventors are careful to record and protect their work so that they can prove who came up with the idea first.

During the 1800s, a very useful recording tool was invented—the camera. Now people could capture important moments for all to see. Early cameras were large and hard to use. The later innovations of handheld cameras and easy-to-use film by George Eastman in New York made photography simple enough for everyone to enjoy.

The invention of the airplane by Wilbur and Orville Wright was the first major invention to be fully recorded by the camera. This photo shows Wilbur photographing Orville on a test flight.

Early cameras were bulky and s-l-o-w! People had to sit still for as long as 20 minutes, or the photo would come out blurred. This man's head is being held still with a brace.

In the 1890s, the U.S. Commissioner of Patents suggested he should retire. He thought that every useful thing had been invented!

Writing It Down

Have you ever had a great idea and then forgotten it? Many scientists and inventors carry a notebook or electronic diary everywhere they go. They write down each new idea as soon as they think of it.

Scientists publish information about their experiments in journals. Each journal article, or "paper," is about an idea that a scientist came up with, how he or she tested the idea, and what results were achieved. Every scientist dreams of publishing a paper about an exciting new discovery or invention.

Find Out More!

1. Many of the inventions in this book begin with *tele-*. Find out what this prefix means. Can you think of other words that begin with *tele-*?

2. This book could not have been printed without the great work of many inventors. What can you find out about the inventions of ink, paper, and the printing press?

> To find out more about the ideas in *Eye on Invention*, do research at a library or on the Internet.

Index

appliances	12–13
computers	16–17
electricity	7–9, 17
flight	5–6, 14–15, 22
light	6, 8–9
mass production	11
moving images	18–19
sound	16–19
transportation	5–6, 11, 14–15, 22